The Truck Driver's Daughter

Poems By
Denise R. Weuve

for my mother, who did it on her own, before it was in fashion.

CONTENTS

ACKNOWLEDGMENTS

Grateful acknowledgment is made to the following journals in which these poems originally appeared—perhaps in a slightly different form: *Bop Dead City*, *Cadence Collective*, *Carnival Literary Magazine*, *Curio Poetry*, *Emerge Literary Journal*, *Eunoia Review*, *First Literary Review-East*, *Genre*, *Gutter Eloquence*, *Mojave River Review*, *Napalm and Novocain*, *Pearl*, *Pyrokinection*, *Red River Review*, *San Pedro River Review*, *Sheila-na-Gig*, *Silverbirch Press*, and *What's Your Sign?*

I would like to thank those who have assisted, indulged, and inspired me on the way to completing this collection. You each know how much you have meant to me, but for the record my gratitude to: Cathy Smith Bowers, Shivani Mehta, Tobi Cogswell, G. Murray Thomas, Daniel Romo, Cindy Hoochman, Batty, and Alan Barkhordar.

I'm a travelin' man
I've made a lot of stops all over the world
And in every port I own the heart
Of at least one lovely girl

From the Song "Travelin' Man,"
written by Jerry Fuller ©1961

When My Mother Danced

My father left for the weekend,
this time to Seattle.
As usual she ironed
his cotton blue shirt and pressed
a perfect crease in work jeans.
Too neat
for a man who would spend the entire
time behind the wheel.

My grandmother came over
from the community center
where she played Bingo,
and was the proud winner
of four Farmer John's chickens.
To celebrate, my mother
removed the plastic doily
from the pop top stereo
and music played.
She danced with my Grandmother,
dipping and turning her
as if she were a music box ballerina,
the way my father would have
with my mother, if he were ever around.

They were two women
who did not need permission
to pin their paisley dresses
above their knees, whisper
curse words, or dance in each other's arms.
They placed the coffee table on the sofa

and showed off the Sugar Foot,
Twisted until they wore holes
through the carpet, then Two-Stepped
to Ricky Nelson's "Traveling Man."

Duplex

for Gregory Johnson

1

Stirring your tomato soup counterclock-
Wise, I saw a tear sneak out of your eye,
the first tear noticed from a boy not socked
in the jaw on the playground.
                              Next door, lies
sifted through the walls like powder sugar
coating your bruised ginger skin, promising
she would not spend
                              the school day at Deb's Bar
again, come home around three, stumbling
over third-grade friends assembled for juice,
orange or apple, neither after she
started swinging. You laughed, called her footloose
fancy-free, just misguided or angry
with the way you tucked your shirt corners in;
awkward, sloppy, an unforgiven sin.

2

Refuge was in our house where my mother
fed you cookies, soup, and vitamin D
milk, not the instant kind that bothered
your stomach. She'd pat your back, a decree
that these horrible things never happen
here in the duplex knotted against yours,
where the children were
                              scarred silent by then.
The relentless threat of violence devoured

our air. *A man's going to beat the hell*
out of you, little girl, she'd say, meaning,
just like my father had done to her, cell
by cell of her body.
                    Then your leaving
floored me. Why go back? *She's my mother,* you'd
say, walking out, and somehow I understood.

little 15

your black fingernails
          and purple hair
could send a young girl
          screaming, but I,
in catholic school
          uniform, was
green for you. wanted
          your easy life,
our alley nights with
          southern comfort.
while nuns preached gospel
          spells to me, you,
the prodigal son
          pocketed your
pick from the fat of
          women's thighs, and
brought gifts of sooty
          eyeliner and
peroxide to me.
          i remember
the neon nights, the
          back of your ford,
and the sinking, when
          the riotous
living was ending.
          your roots began
bleeding and the farm
          boy surfaced. soon
the banshees would mean
          nothing to us
and *o.m.d.* would
          be three over

used letters; i
        never made you
say good-bye. how could
        i? pushed and shoved
your father had bought
        new silken robes
and killed the fattest
        calf for your return.

Cycles

My sister counts
the days to rehab
on a calendar
instead of her cycle.
We drive past the center.
> *--See there, the green bricks,*
> *that's where I'll be*
>> *--I'll visit you*
> *--bring my kids*

And I promise this,
another lie shared
between sisters
like lipstick—
the frosty kind.

We rode to her dealer, and
I waited in her Honda,
windows rolled up,
sunk deep down in the seat
for over a half hour,
until she came down the stairs,
tucking her V-neck
T-shirt into her
Hip-hugging jeans,
her purse fuller.
> *You want? It could be stronger*

And I do, feel the sharp
cramps that come
with longing, but saw her
two years ago
coming down

scratching her face,
her skin collecting
under her fingernails
and she bled—
the blood that is mine
still staining her hands.

Jesse James 78

From April 8th in the front seat of a silver mist Camry
I knew I wanted to be the reason AA didn't work.
Sober people are unnatural, like Icarus ascending
through a misty moonlit night forever on Step 4,
listing his fearless moral inventory straight into relapse.

whore

she is doing it again—
leaving behind
the needles,
her discarded lovers,
one after another,
a trail to her other
side, the side
that is not a mother,
the side that never
wanted to be a
mother.
her breasts have
always been dry,
empty sex toys
she displays
on merchant marine
ships like green cards
for the Asian sailors.
she will sit in bars
for hours, sending
watered down drinks
to men eating balut.
the duckling ready
to hatch, but boiled
just before the bill
could form.
It makes her ill
watching them peel
away the flesh,
place the still-closed

eyes on their tongues.
she forgives them all,
those mouths being
the ones she will kiss
for 50 dollars,
300 if she stays
the night.
her daughter will
figure this out soon,
drop the needles
from the air
like Chinese fortune
sticks that explain her fate,
then spend the night
with a Georgian boy
ask for 20 dollars
knowing this is what
all women do
in smaller amounts.

The Haircut

Maybe my mother
wanted to capture
the clock, so she
crooked the camera,
aiming for the corner,
barely keeping
my two-year-old
brother in frame.
Just maybe she knew
he was already
creeping out through
the negative,
projecting
to seventeen,
when he could jump
from the barber's chair
and let his hair grow
to the length he wanted.
Or maybe she just
wanted to know
it was ten after four
the day she lost control.

Abel

The Story will end like this, dear brother.
I will take you there,
a barren farmland,
as dry as your wife, the day you don't return.

Then I will always have your screams
echoing through the crops in the city I build.
The ascending fist welts on your chest,
damning as a garden apple, twice bitten.

Poor mother, how she always
wrapped her perfume around you—
the sweetest honeysuckle—
like a shroud for survival.

Useless now. Where your blood colors
the earth, I shall blossom.
My head turned to God,
the mocking daffodil.

And you will know my only promise,
brother dear, I will be your keeper.
Keep you six feet under.
Keep you begging for God's favor.

Kinder der Landstrasse

Late Thursday night my mother dragged my brother and me two duplexes back to Alice Stagg's apartment. I pretended we were traveling gypsies. Tied a towel around my waist and danced to the banging at the front door. My mother hid in the kitchen, as your demands to be let in became a campfire song your gypsy daughter stomped in rhythm with. Your begging for forgiveness became a chant, a curse, a hex my mother feared. She hid her gypsy children, *Jenisch*, in shadow filled corner of a bedroom from you, and the Swiss. The Swiss wanted to eliminate the gypsies by stealing their children, and giving them to wholesome families. At least then the children would have a chance. All gypsies were crazy, even the German Roma gypsies, the Swiss could see that through their holes. You ignored their stereotypes of insanity, as you threw beer bottles, one after another, against the alumina siding. I listened to them ring out their descent and shatter like a family crashing at 11pm on a Thursday evening.

Let's be clear, father: I wanted to be an orphan.

Love,
Zigenare dotter.

The Oracle of Daisy Street

My mother was the Oracle of Daisy Street.
In purple polyester
she divined prophecies with playing cards
the same way gypsies would.
Intricate tarot were costly
when the truth could be predicted
with a 25-cent pack of Bicycle cards.

One by one she flipped the cards
for neighbors, who showed up in house dresses
looking for tea and destiny,
coffee cake if it was the beginning of the month.
She'd puff a celestial telling in a raspy voice
through drags of Marlboro Lights.

10 of diamonds, unexpected financial luck is on your way
And so it was.
A welfare check and dead husband's Social Security,
both arriving on the third.

4 of clubs, change for someone you love.
And so it was.
A heroin-addicted son free on probation
back in the garage by nightfall to start anew.

2 of hearts, for you, love late in life.
And so it was.
That night a man sitting at the end of the bar
professes love and never leaves you.

The Ace of Spades, no one wanted to see:
foretold of death, but not whose.

On these days, women went home not believing in my mother
until 3a.m. knocks on their front doors.

I envied these women who were given the grace of cards,
allowed fate or chance to step in.
I was never given that luxury.
Mother prophesied for me through the Gods.
They slipped into her head late in the evening,
I'd see them shifting behind her blue eyes
as their words spilled out of her mouth,

No one will love you
Not without beating you.
The possession phase would die
just before the 11 o'clock news.
I wanted to be resentful
but the Gods
can possess anyone.

What Can't Be Told

I want to tell you   that I never saw the comforter   crumpled at
the end of the bed   cowering   waiting for the
next blow   permanent creases   in sheets I gripped as if
there were a chance   I could crawl out   from under you
were never seen   I didn't pull the sheets   like any Sunday
morning for cleaning   stuff them into a black hefty bag and
listen   to them collide against walls of the trash chute the red
wrap dress   the one with the petal-like opening just above the knee
the one you called striking   has not been shredded   with salad
shears not a solitary day was found sitting in the dark refusing to
answer doors calls   texts   just in case   a 6-foot man with
shoulders   like safe tomorrows and tight gray t-shirt
outlining chiseled oppression   doesn't make me shiver   men in
their 30's   of your race   don't disgust me cause me to
avoid eye contact   the new comforter isn't less
frillyless inviting   more beige   simple blends in   never to
be noticed   I want to tell you no man   ever   has   to
worry   about the steak knife between my mattress and box spring

Human Anatomy Parts

None of my parts are original,
one of my kidneys
belongs to a 35 year-old Hispanic woman
whose name I will never know
nor how she died.
Maybe a traffic accident,
or a lover waiting beneath
her bed next to dust bunnies
and regrets forging their way
into bullets with gunpowder and tomorrows.
The other kidneys I leave where they were
except I turn them to face each other,
sad formaldehyde guinea pigs
commiserating about a life they never got to live.

My eyes stolen from a father
that disappears at seven
in the evening.
These sapphire eyes
wander truck driver style
searching for the next rest stop
or diner to forget there is a daughter
358 miles away.

The liver I have moved
to the center of my chest,
it ferments in vodka
becomes sauerkraut strong,
like the grandfather
whose hate sat so long

it had to swing from a basement beam
on a Thursday night.
My heart rest where the spleen once was,
enlarged, filled with a bacteria strain
whose origin puzzles even the devil,
as he puffs on filtered Marlboro,
talks of his yesterdays
with Gabriel and Michael:
Back then, they decided what parts belonged to whom
placed crystal vocal cords into humans
so we could praise our creators.
Once we all loved.

Reading Carver

I drink a greyhound
I can't keep up with,
whiskey so bitter
it calls up that man,
the one,
who wore his wedding band
while he held me at the waist.
So we drank,
Jack Daniels, Smirnoff,
anything left in the cupboard,
while his wife was away,
her mother ill in Iowa.
We read Carver,
cutting our losses
into our skin,
dog-earing the pages
his characters drank on
knowing someone else was dying,
someone else's liver
was going.
Between the swigs he grumbled
    Carver had it
    the less said, the better.
So we say nothing.
Me wanting to know
when his wife would return.
Him wanting to know
when I would leave
and I already had.

The Scientist's Siren

He stirred a composition of neon,
gold flakes, and silicon
seven times clockwise
and created an antidote

to loneliness—a woman.
When she walked, he measured
time by the sway of her hips
and love by the pitch of her voice.

A voice that made copper roses appear
and morning glories crawl up the walls.
She sang, praising his hands
how they had balanced life,

and how they lightly pressed
against her back
as he waltzed her around the lab
not paying attention

to the iodine spilled
on the floor.
Yet oxygen in the room
seemed thinner after a while.

He longed for his work,
moving beakers, attempting to melt
silver and lead at the same temperature.
Her voice made it impossible

to concentrate on creating
another, without a voice.

He put her in the east corner of the room
between Bunsen burners and microscopes

that had lost their magnifying power,
and kept his hands in motion
from acid compounds to liquid golds.
Still she sang,

from not far behind,
and it was reassuring,
as long as she didn't
knock over chemicals arranged

in alphabetical order.
The music became softer,
a background to his life,
further removed from her body.

He does not know when she disappeared
but remembers waking in silence.

3:08 a.m.

There will be handcuffs,
there always is
a full body search,
invasive and belittling,
a minor assault,
his Israeli Army-trained hands
wrapped about the throat,
the thumbs driving down
on the trachea,
then the strained breathing
that startles his narcissistic palms.
He'll let go,
his crime incomplete
find another way to chalk-outline
the dignity
that entered with
this hollow body.
He'll stare at the mark
around the neck
like a foolishly tied red ribbon
or a collar he
didn't fasten soon enough.
It will be days before
the full extent
of the damage is realized,
before every breath
feels like a bruise.

Out of Love

Aquella mujer bella que un loco por odio destruyo . . .
From a painting at the MOLAA

First he removed her feet,
there would be no more midnight departures,
placed them on the shoe rack
between lavender sandals and red stilettos
then he removed the knees
to end her bending back and away.

Here is where it all broke down:
He loved her hands,
the deep lines that scored her knuckles,
how those hands molded to the shape
of only his face
knowingly traveling the shadow of his jaw
well after 5 p.m.
he could not be without
those palmy pillows.

He'd not have them trace the cleft chin of a fireman
or tangle with a calloused guitar player.
these became more important to keep
than her tramping feet
or meandering knees.

He twisted them
counterclockwise
at the wrist,
each turn recording his hate
till it was dismantled.

Now what was wholly beautiful
lies in pieces
a woman,
his woman,
destroyed.

He Wants Only

women
with wide hips
and crossed eyes.
He knows the truth,
no one looks twice
at the unsightly—
unless making sure
it's real.

Think of Perseus
his fascination
with Medusa,
how her reflection
in that golden shield
made him cringe
yet he glimpsed once more
before he fucked her
through and through,
a quick plunge of the sword.

He is smart,
my lover,
reminding me how I grow
with dandelion frenzy
from the blood of Medusa,
eyes slender Helens,
while taking me home
where only my heart
turns to stone.

Fire Eater

In Malibu
the fires
are finally

out, but ashes
hover
like fine despair.

Somebody's hopes
cover
my Toyota

and I dust them
away
the way you once

did me. I
should not
care when I hear

you are engaged
yet my
stomach tightens

on the smoke that
is your
ghostly presence

still on my love
seat. How
quickly could I

extinguish
your new
woman's burning

if I told of
our bed
smoldering lust

into love. Tongues
darting
like blue flames

into each other's
mouths
'til we ignited.

I always knew
I was
strong enough

to eat fire. Would
she leave
you? Cold gray groom

at the altar
the way
you left me for

an icy North,
when hot
embers still burned

in my stomach.
I am
fine now, gutted,

an empty house,
fodder
for men to search

through. Still, I wish
you the
best, but warn you,

not all women
can eat
fire and survive.

As Good As New

That day when the neighbors
banged on the front door
for their noon coffee
and cake, I followed
instructions, told them
my mother, and you, Sister,
were at a baby shower.

Even when you came back
later that evening sick
with tears, Mother said
the shower was fine.
Swallowed Catholic
pride like the birth control
pills you misplaced, and never

spoke of that day again.
Not even when your boyfriend
pulled up in the cherry
Chevy, said any
other time he would
have dipped into his
savings, but this he couldn't pass.

Lilith

for edward hanson

How strange that you, my friend,
come stationed with your own cross,
your palms bleeding because your heart
cannot. You tell me of women
leaving one after another like months

gone by too quickly. You wrap yourself
in pages of the Bible; Samson had Delilah,
Adam had Eve. Why so hard for you?
And this is how you will live, church
bulletins scattered around your room

where used condoms should be, all
because you believe the woman for you
will fit like a missing rib. But
what of Lilith, her long night-bred hair.
Her sleek body demanding space,

her eyes wide almonds, grasping life
quicker than any man formed
of the earth. Can you not
imagine it? A woman aware
of the violence of your sex, how it

encompasses the world, yet willing
to open her legs and let you in. Or
are you just scared that a woman
like that could make you worship her.

Endangered

Her back is lizard skin
drawing blood
from gloved hands,
needing to domesticate.
These hands,
with new scabs, trick her into
rooms with fresh sheets
and lifetime rates, never hourly.
There'll be a Bible
on the dresser top
instead of a rat in the corner
gawking with Polaroid eyes,
turning his nose up at her
drug store perfume.
She'll have to trade in her ripped jeans
for cotton poly blend gowns.
She'll attempt a midnight run
where desert winds blow
and those hands will catch her.
They'll skin her,
make shoes
or a beige-colored purse
that matches any outfit,
even a faded house dress.

Rain

For Yvonne Sham-Shackleton

Since you returned home,
it has rained once or twice,
hard petal-like drops
scrubbing the streets clean
of oil leaks and old leaves.
In my back yard, the hopscotch frame
is gone as well, those purple squares
we drew with my niece's thumb-thick chalk,
disappeared as if we never called turns,
tossed nickel markers, or pirouetted
in 180-degree twirls.
                        For a moment
we were nine, did not bother
with make-up to entice boys,
let our ponytails bounce,
believed that the pink plastic heart-
shaped rings were wedding bands
encircling us to each other
through knee scrapes,
Chinese jump ropes,
and roughed-up rag dolls;
a closeness husbands cannot touch.

Marlboro Lights After Sex

He lied.
Said he didn't smoke.
Now he stands in the corner near the dresser,
pants loose,
unbuckled belt,
Marlboro Light glowing
as ashes descend.
Crushing the cigarette, a smile
creeps through his late-night stubble
and he comes back to bed,
shifts beneath the sheets
wrapping his arms around me,
fingers interlocking.
He doesn't smell like smoke
or a day lost in red tape
that found him in the red
but of a man that is Tide-clean,
freshly minted
in a mix of linen and cotton;
a man of expensive cologne
that has been muddled in the scent of sex.
He sleeps.
There is peace here
in the rise and fall of his chest,
before I learn
all the other lies
that make this man.

Heredity

The moles you search out
on your arm still have not
given way to disease.
But this time it is no phantom
lump in your breast.
This time it is eating you
from the inside out,
malignant as all four
children combined.
You curse
the four men you've loved
who left children,
blame them for the cancer
poisoning your uterus.
When the doctor guts you,
promises it is all gone
you still feel them,
deep inside, the husbands
digging in you,
planting their hate,
bluer than any despair
in your children's eyes.
You have watched them
grow into their fathers,
one's drug addiction,
one with alcoholic binges,
another just a thief,
and this one,
blessed female
who too often walks
as pigeoned as you into
the callous hands of men.

You leave her death
neatly wrapped in yearly
visits to the gynecologist,
scraped from the inside out.
Each year she reaches out,
head tilted to the doctor's whisper,
and does not breathe
long enough to hear,
you are not your mother.

ABOUT THE AUTHOR

Denise R. Weuve is a Pushcart Prize nominee who resides in Southern California. Her poetry has been published in numerous journals and she is the recipient of the *Donald Drury Award* and annual *Sheila-Na-Gig Poetry Prize*. In 2014 she founded *Wherewithal,* a poetry journal, while maintaining her editing position with *Cease, Cows,* completing her MFA at Queens University of Charlotte, and teaching Creative Writing and British Literature to Southern California teens at Cerritos High School.